ARE THESE REALLY MY PANTS?

ARE THESE REALLY MY PANTS?

THE FUNNY LESSONS I'VE LEARNED IN TRYING
TO WEAR THE TITLE "CULT LEADER"

ERIC LUDY

Copyright © 2015 by Eric Ludy

All rights reserved. No part of this book may be reproduced in any form without prior permission from the publisher, except for brief quotations.

Scripture taken from the King James Version®. Public Domain.

ISBN 9781943592067 (paperback)
ISBN 9781943592166 (ebook)

ELLERSLIE PRESS
655 Southwood Lane
Windsor, CO 80550
Ellerslie.com

Published in the United States of America.
First Edition, 2015
Second Edition, 2016

ERICLUDY.COM

To my dear wife who gets the privilege of standing in these gigantic pants right alongside me. These pants have brought us together in a beautiful way, and I'll always be thankful for that.

CONTENTS

9   Prologue

15   How to Get Your Own Pair of Gigantic Pants

21   Where to Go to Get Those Massive Pants

27   Should You Feel Bad Having the Pants If You Didn't Actually Pay for Them?

33   So, How Does One Actually Wear A Pair of Pants This Big?

35   What Can You Do With the Extra 124 Inches of Denim?

39   So, Who Do These Pants Really Belong To?

43   So, What's Next for the Guy with the Thirty-Two Inch Waistline?

PROLOGUE

If you've checked out the cover photo for this book, you may be wondering where I picked up such an amazing pair of pants.

Well, it's hard to explain.

You see, they are sort of a gift. They don't fit well, but my mom always taught me that when you receive a gift it's only right and respectful to try the duds on and do your best to smile even when they fall down to your ankles in a heap. (Okay, maybe that's not a direct quote.)

I've received some awkward gifts in my life. The velour v-neck sweater from Grandma, the "I Love Nooma Videos, Don't You?" t-shirt, and the book entitled "Your Best Life Now" all rank as storied examples of gifts that begat a panicky pause, a fidgety laugh, and then a strained thank-you. But the title of "cult leader" — generously bestowed upon me by some rather sketchy, unnamed sources — was truly a unique test to my gift-receiving etiquette. Just like opening up a festively wrapped gift box and pulling out an enormous pair of pants that are 124 sizes too large, this generous and thoughtful "gift" has put me in a very awkward position. Thankfully, due to my mom's faithful training, I've become skilled at receiving supremely embarrassing gifts like this one with a big toothy smile and an excited proclamation of "oh, you shouldn't have!" — while expertly suppressing the urge to break into incredulous laughter and quickly surveying the room for Candid Camera.

The late Andre the Giant was a gigantic man. His pants were huge, too — I'm guessing a 156-inch waistline. These jumbo pants I received are so ill-fitting that they very well may have been his, stolen from the WWF museum. They are downright massive. And, to be honest, my 32-inch waistline just doesn't offer the hip support for these mongo drawers. So though I can hold them up and smile for the camera, "gargantuan" and "super-awkward" are the two words that come to mind every time I do. Quite simply, as thoughtful as the gift was, these "cult leader" pants just don't come close to fitting me. But I keep repeating my dear mother's words: "Eric, when you receive a gift, it's only right and respectful…"

So, though the "gift" is making my daily duties a bit strained, I'm getting better each and every day in trying to graciously accept the big heap of denim piled unceremoniously at my ankles. (And don't worry — I always wear my trusty Nike workout shorts while trudging around in the ill-fitting pants. After all, as an old saying goes, "One cannot rely on pants that are 124 sizes too big to keep one's legs respectably covered!" Or, at least, I think that is how the old saying goes. Or did I just make that up?)

Cult leaders are historically bad dudes. The term conjures up pictures of Kool-Aid, white robes, military compounds, and Waco, Texas. Typically one might try to stay away from such infamous terminology. But, in my case, it came and found me. According to the sketchy sources who bestowed this "cult leader" title upon me, I am the ideal fit for these huge metaphorical pants, this rather infamous moniker. I wasn't looking for these pants, believe me. But the pants, I suppose, were needing a sturdy pair of legs to call home, and so, for lack of finding any meaty legs to cling to, they attempted to grab onto my skinny ones instead.

So just why am I the wrong guy to wear these ginormous pants? Well, correct me if I'm wrong, but aren't cult leaders supposed to be the controlling type? You know, the brilliantly insane, hyper-manipulative sort — guys that struggle with an "I'm the Messiah" complex?

That's definitely not me. I am not brilliant *or* insane. I am not controlling or stricken with a Messiah-complex. And I do not own any white robes or Kool-Aid. In fact, I am so opposite of these descriptions that I am rather shocked I could possibly garner such a title from anyone. However, I've decided to consider it an honor. I mean, the questionable sources who have attempted to bestow this title upon me couldn't possibly have meant that I'm a "cult leader" like Jim Jones or David Koresh, did they? Of course not.

My take is that they wanted so desperately to encourage me in my ministry and my stand for truth in this generation that they quickly stated the approbation they felt was most complimentary.

Here's probably how it happened. They had three competing ideas in their heads. Eric is a "kind" leader. Eric is a "cool" leader. And Eric is a "full-tilt" leader.

They couldn't decide which one to say, and they were probably in a big hurry. So when they went to declare their encouragement, they accidentally blended the three descriptions together and came up with "Eric is a k-coo-cult leader." As a communicator, I understand how these foibles can happen.

I've thought about it and I've come to a decision. Since it was obviously an attempt at a compliment, I'm going to receive it that way (just like Grandma's velour v-neck sweater). So, for this little book, I'm going wear these jumbo pants around my ankles with a smile (and with my trusty Nike workout shorts properly in place!).

Since I am more the tail-wagging golden retriever sort of guy than the great ape who beats his chest and commands his females into submission, I'm guessing that, if I really am a cult leader, then one of two things must be true:

1. Either cult leaders are actually pretty nice folk, and all our negative stereotypes throughout the years were wrong and it's high time we got excited about these guys.

2. Or, I'm the worst cult leader ever in the history of the world.

Either option makes me smile.

But, the one thing I can't get past is the fact that, no matter how hard I try to fit into these grandiose pants, they keep piling up at my ankles. I just can't help but think that maybe these pants were designed to fit someone a little...um...how can I say this? Hmmm. Someone who actually fits the pants.

Prologue

So, how did I receive these pants...er...get called this wonderful title of "cult leader," you ask?

Well, it certainly wasn't my life's ambition. I was like every other young boy who dreamed of being a Neil Armstrong, a GI Joe, or the next Tom Cruise. Cult leader wasn't even in my top one hundred options. I may not fit these pants very well, but just think how rare and unique a pair of pants with a 156-inch waistline is? I bet these puppies are probably worth a fortune, especially if they really did come from the WWF hall of fame.

This great...um..."honor" has moved me to take pen to paper (or fingers to keyboard) to elucidate the amazing things I've learned in this journey of becoming a ...well...a guy with a gigantic pair of awkward pants around my ankles.

There may be others of you out there who wish to follow my example and acquire a big pile of denim all your own. So I figured maybe I should write down a few pointers.

I've broken this little book into seven short lessons. These are the lessons I've learned in my journey to getting Andre the Giant's pants as my very own. I sheepishly must admit, even as I begin to write, that I feel unworthy of such a rare and lofty title. As the Apostle Paul declared himself the "least of all the saints," in like manner, I'm certainly the least of all the world's "kind, cool, and full-tilt" leaders today.

I realize that many of you may have dreamed of having such a pile of denim at your ankles as I currently have at mine. Well, it's my goal in this book to show you how to do just that.

My mind drifts to the story in Matthew chapter five

where Jesus is sharing what we as Christians are to do when someone asks for our tunic. He says we ought to give them our cloak as well. Well, I wish you to know that I take that concept seriously. So, if anyone asks for my jumbo pants, I will even throw in my red polka-dotted socks, so that you can walk away with your own awkward and ultra-spacious outfit.

Here's to clothes that fit!

Leaping for joy…in spite of the pile around my ankles!

Ellerslie Campus, Windsor, Colorado

1

HOW TO GET YOUR OWN PAIR OF GIGANTIC PANTS

The First Lesson: The Idiot Preacher Gets the Prize

Huge pants. I'm sure you are wondering how to get yourself a pair.

If you have a 32-inch waist like me, then there are certain pairs of pants that fit. And others... not so much.

For instance:

"Eric, you are an idiot!" (Now that's a pair of pants, that though it be a bit itchy, at least might fit a slim waistline.)

"Eric, you have bad breath!" (I'd be embarrassed, but hey, it could fit.)

"Eric, your opinion on speaking in tongues stinks!" (I don't agree, but at least it falls within the bounds of a 32-inch waistline.)

"Eric, you preach way too loud!" (That one is just plain true.)

"Eric, your eschatology is absolute nonsense! Your messages are too long! And your soteriological viewpoint is an embarrassment to the pastorate!" (I'd be a bit hurt, but at least those are pairs of pants that could conceivably be in the 32-inch category.)

But, "Eric, you are a cult leader" — that's a totally different story. It's sort of like naming Winnie the Pooh *People Magazine's* "Sexiest Man Alive." It would be quite humorous, but not very accurate. It's like eleven inches of frosting on the top of a little tiny cupcake. It's too much.

So, what was my secret, you ask, to circumventing all logic and reason and being named "Sexiest Man Alive"...er...I mean "cult leader"?

In a way, I guess I cheated the system. I got eleven inches of frosting on my teeny cupcake whereas a quarter-inch of the stuff is typical and reasonable. So, how did I do it?

Well, to get the extra frosting on your cupcake you can't play by the rules of normal social order. For a 32-inch waist to receive the honor of Andre-the-Giant-style-pants, mild violations of political incorrectness will simply not do, and everyday Christian uncoolness won't cut it.

I can tell you how I got 'er done.

I started preaching — preaching strong, and preaching loud.

There is something about bold preaching that pumps up everyone's opinions like an inflatable jumpy castle. Preaching is jarring to people's souls; it's completely unexpected. It forces a decision, a response. And often, as I've found, it leads to people upgrading their perception of your real waistline and how much denim you deserve. It pumps up their vision of your prowess, whether that be good or bad.

So, all that said, here's the secret for all you fellow 32-inchers, to accessing your very own 156-inch pair of pants:

Preach your heart out!

The idiot preacher, though he may be of slender physique, is able to convince everyone, by means of his idiot preaching, that he is deserving of titles, names, monikers, frosting, and pants much bigger than his actual hip span can reasonably hold up.

Back in the day of William Booth and East End London, the idiot preacher received a rotten tomato to the nose. But today, thanks to the Google generation we live in, the idiot preacher receives something even more exciting: negative online reviews, slanderous blog posts, forum insults, Facebook impersonations, *and* rotten tomatoes to the nose (which usually come in the form of shouts, spittle to the face, death threats, hate letters, and other miscellaneous scuttlebutt).

So, this begs the question: what is an idiot preacher?

I'm sure there are many takes and perspectives on this. But since this is my book, and I am the most honored recipient of these huge pants and this extra dollop of frosting, I will humbly supply you with my personal vantage point on this issue.

NOTE: This definition was exhumed from the *Ludy Dictionary of All Things Uncool*.

IDIOT PREACHER
ˈidēət ˈprēCHər

The guy who preaches too forcibly, teaches too authoritatively, mentions Jesus and the Cross way too much, and doesn't end his sermons at the forty-five minute point.

Now this is a just a rough idea of "the idiot preacher," but I think it will suffice to give us a mental picture. Just think wild hair, wild eyes, and camel skin attire — oh, and you can't forget to include a big, huge Bible whacking people across the face. You know, "Sexiest Man Alive."

I can hear you asking, even begging me, to tell you how one becomes an idiot preacher.

Well, technically speaking, it's not a difficult thing. All you need to do is open your mouth and boldly speak that which is true. But spiritually speaking, there is a bizarre impediment that often stands in the way of us doing this. Being an idiot is easy. Being an idiot preacher is a hard thing. Very few people who desire to walk in this direction are able to. They usually falter after the first few steps. When the mocking jeers reach their ears, they often turn around and return to being the sensible preacher who sounds intelligent, socially appropriate, politically correct, and in full agreement with doctrines that don't call for full abandonment to Jesus Christ.

However, though it is a harder road to walk, this is the secret for those of us with a 32-inch waist. If you want the gargantuan pile of denim at your feet, then you need to learn how to preach. And when you preach, preach like "a fool in love" with the epic beauty, grandeur, majesty, and glory of Jesus Christ and His Cross-work.

2

WHERE TO GO TO GET THOSE MASSIVE PANTS

The Second Lesson: Rile up the Religious Folk

Just a quick heads up: most stores don't carry the 156-inch variety of denim pants. You will not find them at your local Banana Republic, Express, or Macy's. They are special, made-to-order pants. And so, if you are serious about getting yourself a pair, you will need to know where to do your shopping.

I know just the place. It's a little clothier shop on Uppity Boulevard in downtown High-Minded. The store is called *Religiosity*. The last time I checked online, they had some gargantuan pants in stock. After all, that's where I found mine — or, I should say, that's how the pants found me. Technically, they sent me my pair in the mail gratis, so I can't say I've ever been there for a visit. But, from what

I've heard, they are the world's leading maker of gigantic pants of — *ahem* — this sort.

This store has been around for thousands of years. Even Jesus got His pants...er...robes from here. I remember He had some rather large and hefty metaphorical garments that people attempted to thrust on His physique. He was termed a blasphemer, a devil, a false prophet, an illegitimate, and even Beelzebub — all rather salty descriptions. But every single one of these garments, if you looked at the tag, would say, "Handmade with Zeal at Religiosity."

Religiosity has been shipping out pants (or robes) for free since long before the days of Christ. They are solely funded by the deep pockets of spiritual pride and are a purely not-for-profit venture. They share because they...uh ...care.

So, you ask, how do you get on their list for a shipment?

The word for it is "rile." It's an interesting word, so let's define it:

RILE
/rīl/

To greatly annoy someone.

To get your own pair of gigantic pants, you can't just be an idiot preacher. You also need to rile the people who ship out the jumbo pants.

Though my efforts were not purposeful, I, Eric Ludy (the tail-wagging, golden retriever), accidentally "riled" the religious folk that run the Religiosity shop.

Unlike many of you, I wasn't actually trying to get a big pair of pants shipped my way. I honestly wasn't trying to doing any "riling." But riling I did.

So, since I've become so adept at this riling thing, let me teach you how to do it.

Pssst. Come close. I don't want to say this too loud, because if it gets out far and wide, then Religiosity will run out of inventory way too fast and you just might not get your own pair. So, lean in and listen closely.

If you want to do some riling, you need to know the buttons to push. And Religiosity has a series of buttons that, if pushed just right, go a long way to getting you your own pair of pants. It's sort of like using a coupon code in an online store. Just enter this code and voila! you've got yourself a free pair of jumbo jeans.

You see, Religiosity is a watchdog operation that is always looking for the next 156-inch waist. But, if you don't have a 156-inch waist, then "pushing the buttons" is the only way past their red tape.

Here's a short list of buttons that worked for me:

"Hey, world! I'm not a five-point Calvinist."

I know this sounds harmless (and for some might not even make sense), but when mixed just right with a loud voice and strong preaching, it pushes some kind of button in the back offices of Religiosity.

"The entire Bible is about One Thing, points to One Thing, and reveals One Thing — and that One Thing is Jesus Christ and His amazing redemptive work on the Cross!"

Again this might sound like a rather obvious statement, but Religiosity holds onto a lot of pet doctrines that get stomped on when you preach (or push) this button boldly.

"Jesus demands that you give up your entire life to follow Him!"

Yes, this is just good old fashioned Christianity, but it does wonders in bothering the workers at the Religiosity shop. As connoisseurs of 156-inch waistlines, they often lose sight of good old-fashioned Christianity and only see what's wrong with other Christians instead of noticing that eleven inches of icing just doesn't quite fit on top of that little cupcake.

Jesus did some riling in His day. He seemed to purposely go out of His way to stomp on the long-held traditions, pet doctrines, and intellectual chewing bones of the entire Religiosity staff. And it worked really well for Him. He was shipped out His very own wardrobe, hand-stitched by the riled workers on Uppity Boulevard, almost the very next day.

So, it appears that this "push their buttons" technique is a time-tested idea.

Now, don't get me wrong. I honestly think that the workers at Religiosity have something wonderful to offer the Body of Christ. They just seem to be a bit off-kilter. After all, there really are blasphemers, devils, false prophets, and really bad dudes that are operative on the earth today. And marking them as such is a noble task. But quite often, the religious folk at Religiosity don't mind these blubber-bellied waistlines as much as they do the idiot preachers, because the idiot preachers poke at the personal sin of those working at Religiosity, reprove them for having a form of godliness and denying the power thereof, and ask them to repent and yield their lives wholly and completely to Jesus Christ.

And that, my friends, is how to push the wrong... er... *right* buttons.

So, for all you aspiring to gain your own personal mongo pants like mine, here's the deal: speak truth and don't fear the bad opinion of the religious folk, and I'm confident that you too can one day have a massive pile of denim heaped at your ankles. (Be sure to purchase those stylish Nike workout shorts in advance — you'll need 'em!)

Remember when Barabbas and Jesus (the greatest idiot preacher to ever walk this earth) stood before the religious folk on Uppity Boulevard? The Religiosity group was given the choice of who to give the pants to, and who to let go free. They let Barabbas, the "156-waist-lined" murderer, go free while crowning Jesus as the man worthy of ridicule.

Standing up with Jesus is not always easy. But you do get a free pair of pants — and so much more — in the deal.

3

SHOULD YOU FEEL BAD HAVING THE PANTS IF YOU DIDN'T ACTUALLY PAY FOR THEM?

The Third Lesson: Don't Accept the Title Quickly

If I didn't pay for the pants, should I return them to the sender?

I can understand the concern. After all, you labored long and hard to get noticed by the staff at Religiosity and now you are feeling a bit guilty receiving something in the mail that is much too big for your waistline. I mean, that's a lot of good material going to waist...er...*waste!*

This may be difficult to hear, but, yes, you really should return them to the sender. It is wholly inappropriate for you to receive that much denim on a false claim and without proper remuneration.

The grand examples in history show us that when great honors are offered freely, they should not be received hastily or without appeal.

For instance, William Wallace was offered the crown of Scotland three times. He rejected it every time.

George Washington turned down the office of President when it was served up to him by the Continental Congress.

So, if Religiosity ships you a free pair of jumbo pants with a 156-inch waistline that you didn't pay for and that are not your size, then instantly package them back up and return them to their home address on Uppity Boulevard.

Hear me. It is simply not right for you to have a pair of pants that belong to someone else. I realize that you may want all that free denim, but it's just not yours to have.

"So, Eric," you say, "how is it then that you still have this gigantic pair of pants heaped at your ankles? You seem to be asking us to ship back something that you yourself are holding on to?"

That's a great point. For, if you look at the cover of this book, I still have these awkward pants. But it's not for any lack on my part of shipping pants back to the Religiosity warehouse. In fact, I've spent a lot of money in postage stamps attempting to send these babies home.

You see, there's a funny twist to sending back these pants to the Religiosity warehouse.

When you ship pants back, you will soon find that the workers at Religiosity don't like to take pants back that they shipped out. I'm not sure if it is a restocking problem on their end or what, but it's just not something they prefer to do.

I know I don't deserve all this excess denim, but no matter how hard I've tried to discuss these matters with customer service, it seems they keep insisting that they are indeed mine. So, after all my attempts of returning, I now in good conscience can stand in and amidst this heap of denim without shame. Yes, they certainly would fit someone else a lot better than they fit me, but hey, I'm now enjoying some guilt-free denim.

Some of you reading this may be interested in finding out when Religiosity first spotted me.

It's ironic, but I've been around doing the same "mischief" for twenty years now (you know, speaking about Jesus, riling people up), and yet it was only five years ago that I received the pants in the mail, a few months before my staff and I launched Ellerslie — our discipleship training program.

I'll never forget opening the box for the first time and seeing the gigantic pants inside. It took me aback. There was a nice little note resting on the top that said something akin to:*

> *These pants are for Eric Ludy!*
>
> *You preach too loud, too long, and too confidently. You don't honor the Sabbath on Saturdays, your wife doesn't wear a head covering, you dare to*

---

* *No, this is not the actual text. This is my family-friendly version, edited for your reading pleasure, and it is a creative mixture of quite a few different notes I received from the staff on Uppity Boulevard.*

> call what you do "discipleship," you like Leonard Ravenhill, you have never officially joined the five-pointers secret society, you speak of the Holy Spirit as if He is still viable today — oh, and you teach about submitting to the Lordship of Jesus Christ as if it were a biblical mandate. How dare you!
>
> Sincerely,
>
> The Ever-Caring Religiosity Staff

It's really nice to receive a gift. But this particular gift sure was odd. Since bestowing on me the title of "cult leader" was rather thoughtful and generous of them, I didn't want to seem rude in sending back the pants. But... these pants were huge. I mean, was I supposed to take this whole thing seriously or was I supposed to break down in hysterical laughter?

As nicely as I could, I packaged these pants back up and returned them to the "Ever-Caring Religiosity staff."

I included a note:[*]

> Dear Ever-Caring Religiosity Staff,
>
> It was kind of you to think of me and to send me these pants and to consider me worthy of such a title as "cult leader." However, as of right now, I don't think that the title is very fitting. For though I am beginning a discipleship training program in June, it is April, and we haven't even started our program yet. To wear "cult leader" pants like these, wouldn't it seem reasonable that there should be some actual students studying

---

[*] hopefully you have caught on by now that the pants are merely a metaphor and not real pants. So, no, this wasn't actually my verbatim response.

under me that I'm doing all sorts of devious things to? So, in all fairness, maybe you should hold onto these pants until I have some time to actually do something worthy of this generous gift.

The tail-wagging Golden Retriever,
Eric Ludy

I thought it strange that in two weeks I had received the pants back in the mail.

The note inside read something akin to:

Dear Eric Ludy,

There was no mistake in sending you the pants. We would appreciate it if you would not send them back. There will be a restocking fee if this happens again.

Sincerely,
The Rather Perturbed Religiosity Staff

I tried sending these gigantic pants back four or five times.

I offered to send them a certified measurement of my waistline, an official doctor's note testifying to my smallish physique, and even provide them with one hundred bona fide witnesses who could attest that I'm actually just a skinny guy with a 32-inch waistline.

But the workers at Religiosity would not have it. I had unwittingly pushed some buttons that triggered the red alert in the back room of the Religiosity offices on Uppity Boulevard, and I guess once the alarm sounds, there is just no way of turning it off.

In the correspondence back and forth, I offered to

pay for plane tickets for the Religiosity staff to come to Windsor, Colorado, and actually see for themselves how oversized these pants really were. But, the simple answer was "We're too busy to take the time to do that."

I understand. I'm a busy guy as well. But in talking with this company it has become quite obvious that their pant-shipping business was possibly needing a new CEO to come in and turn things around. I think Jesus Christ would be perfectly suited for the job.

4

SO, HOW DOES ONE ACTUALLY WEAR A PAIR OF PANTS THIS BIG?

Lesson Four: Only Jesus Can Wear These Duds

I found out the hard way that only Jesus can bear the infamy of these pants.

They are just too big and too itchy for a mere man to walk in. And they are strangely heavy.

The first time I heard that the staff at Religiosity had selected me as a pants distribution recipient, my legs went wobbly and my stomach went hollow. I felt like I was going to fall over and die. My strength vanished. My face went pale.

I realize you would think that I would have leapt for joy and cried out, "Hallelujah!" But, the first few times

I stared at the big pants, they nearly crushed me. Just getting near them brought about a queasiness of soul.

I had to realize that such a pair of pants is simply not able to be worn without serious psychological, emotional, and spiritual damage. It takes Jesus to wear these duds.

He wore my guilt, my shame, my sin, and my cross. But He also showed me that He is the one and only man who can wear these gigantic pants that are currently bunched up around my ankles.

I know it may sound fun to be deemed a cult leader, but it isn't all a bed of roses. It's actually miserable, until you learn to have Him wear the pants.

These pants are heavier than most people think. Every extra inch beyond 32-inch is the equivalent of the weight of baby grand piano. So, 124 extra inches is sort of like attempting to wear a circus of elephants. There isn't a single human alive who can wear that much infamy and keep walking. But, for Jesus Christ, it's as light as a feather.

So, please listen, all those who aspire to bear up these heavy weighted pants of shame: only Christ can do it. So, yield yourselves afresh unto His mighty saving power and grace and allow Him to bear you up amidst the small slurs in order that you might be well-able to endure the larger ones when they land upon you like a thorny crown.

5

WHAT CAN YOU DO WITH THE EXTRA 124 INCHES OF DENIM?

Lesson Five: Manure Makes Great Fertilizer

When we read the book of Job, most of us are quite concerned that God may bring our name up in conversation with the devil the way He did Job's name.

"Hey, Satan! Have you considered my servant Eric?"

Gulp.

We think to ourselves, "Please, God, let me just live under the radar! Don't point me out to the devil!"

Likewise, many Christian leaders today are afraid of awakening the staff of Religiosity to their whereabouts.

They aspire to stay unnoticed and to never set off the alarm in the back offices on Uppity Boulevard. It's known as the C.W.P.P. — *The Christian Witness Protection Program*. It's a great deal. Just sign here on the dotted line, never say this, this, or that, and you too can find safety from the Religiosity mafia.

I can certainly understand this survival instinct. However, there is something lost in this approach to life. Avoiding the negative reviews of the current religious establishment is not going to help change the system.

To change a corrupt system, you will likely need to offend the corrupt system somewhere along the journey.

Though this may sound like a tangent, let's briefly talk about manure.

To most of you, I'm betting that manure is pretty bad stuff. But, though manure smells awful, it also possesses some surprising positive qualities.

It's a wonderful fertilizer. The greenest most luscious plants grow out of manure-tilled soil.

So, if I asked you how you felt about manure, it would be appropriate for you to ask me, "For what use?"

If I said, "Manure as fragrance," I wouldn't blame you for shying away and wrinkling your nose.

If I said, "Manure as fertilizer," I would say you would be crazy *not* to receive a truckload of the stuff and offer up a huge thank-you to those that saw fit to dump it on your life.

My life is richer and more beautiful because of this manure...er...I mean, this accusation of being a cult leader. I am happier, more fit for the ministry, and more adept at allowing Jesus Christ to carry my burdens. The greenest days of my life have emerged in my ministry, marriage, and family, thanks to this manure.

Please don't miss this all important lesson: manure makes amazing fertilizer.

Now, let's get back to those gigantic pants.

There is a tag on each pair of huge pants that Religiosity ships out that reads, "Handmade with Zeal at Religiosity." But if you look at the fine print on each and every tag, it reads, "Made from 100% top quality manure."

You see, these pants, when received as a gift, actually have a heavenly power to enrich and make our life more beautiful because they are made of manure.

Isn't that exciting?

That means if you ever were privileged enough to receive a pair of these pants, that you, in so receiving, now have had 124 inches of excess manure sent to you absolutely free of charge.

Farmers would pay big bucks for this stuff. And you got it all free.

So, take those extra inches of RM (religiosity manure) and make good use of them. Put them to work in your soul and get all the fertilizing value out of them that is possible.

6

SO, WHO DO THESE PANTS REALLY BELONG TO?

Lesson Six: The Real Honor Should Be Paid to Those So Eager to Place it Elsewhere

Let's get a few things straight.

1. I received a pair of pants that is 124 sizes too big for me.

2. When I try to send them back to the store that sent them to me, they sent them back, assuring me that they didn't make a mistake.

3. These pants, even after five years, still don't fit, but remain a big heap piled up at my ankles.

So, this begs the question...

Do these pants actually fit someone?

I've thought about that for the past five years.

In these past five years I have received more than my share of clothing from Religiosity. That's right — it hasn't just been pants. I also received a baseball cap that would only fit the Jolly Green Giant, a pair of driving gloves that were big enough for King Kong — oh, and a pair of shoes that might fit snuggly on the feet of one of those huge cave trolls from *The Lord of the Rings*. These massive relics are all stowed away in my trophy collection and cause chagrined awe every time I see them.

It's interesting what the Bible reveals to us about the staff of Religiosity. It shows us that those sewing the clothes and shipping them out are likely measuring their own waistline in order to make the pattern for the pants, robes, hats, gloves, and shoes.

The staff of Religiosity, in Christ's day, declared Jesus was of the devil, and yet all the while their father *was* the devil (John 8:44). Now that's an ironic twist.

It's sort of like one of those action-packed mystery movies that concludes with a dark twist. The detective who, throughout the movie, was leading the investigation to find the bad guy actually turned out to *be* the bad guy who did the dastardly deed. Do you feel the spine tingle? I sure do!

Often we are afraid of what the staff at Religiosity think, but what if the staff at Religiosity are the actual ones boasting the mythical 156-inch waistline? What if they are the ones who actually fit the pants? What if they are the ones truly deserving of the cult leader title?

Those quick to dish out the accusations are often

purposely throwing people's gazes away from themselves.

Now, that isn't to say that we mustn't ever notate those in our midst who are abusing the Body of Christ and distorting the truth. The Apostle Paul says, "Mark them!" (Romans 16:17). But, when we mark someone, let's make certain that we mark those who actually *should* be marked instead of just sticking hefty pants on those who are just trying to advance the Kingdom of Heaven and bring glory to Jesus Christ.

7

SO, WHAT'S NEXT FOR THE GUY WITH THE THIRTY-TWO INCH WAISTLINE?

Lesson Seven: Keep Swimmin' — Just Keep Swimmin'!

Besides the rich fertilizing qualities, there are a lot of great privileges to having huge pants around.

First, they are a daily reminder of how small, skinny, and weak I really am. After all, we eggheads in the ministry can often fall prey to false notions of our own importance. So, a quick glance every day at these huge pants reminds me that I can't carry this weight without Jesus Christ doing the carrying.

It's funny, but with 124 extra inches of denim lingering nearby it's amazing how "proud" thoughts really don't fit into the script of my life. Imagine Godzilla showing up at the wrong Hollywood set and lumbering onto the scene of a Jane Austen film right in the middle of take. The director cries out, "Cut, cut, cut! Someone get that smelly, green, fire-breathing monstrosity out of here!" It's kind of like that. The oversized pants work like pride repellent within my soul. It's really quite amazing.

Second, these extra inches of shame remind me how important it is to keep fighting this battle over truth. There is nothing quite like a massive load of manure-infused denim to get your head back in the game. I know they are merely pants, but, in a bizarre way, they shout at me kind of like a fiery boxing coach:

"Come on, Ludy! The devil's scared. You've got him on the ropes. His left eye is swelling up. He's throwing cheap shots. So keep hitting him where he's hurting! Pour it on, Ludy! Hit 'em harder! Don't let up!"

It's ironic, but Religiosity sends me the denim in hopes of getting me to pipe down. But all the denim does is get me talking louder. After all, in my mind, I figure I must be saying something important; otherwise the bells in the back offices of Religiosity wouldn't be doing so much ringing.

And thirdly, these extra 124 inches are providing great exercise for my soul.

Since you can't use this massive denim monstrosity as actual pants, I've found that they make for a great pool. I mean, you can literally swim in 'em. And when filled with the "living water" of the Holy Spirit, these duds make me want to shout, "Watch out, Mr. Phelps! With all the practice I'm getting on my freestyle, I'm likely your greatest threat come the next Olympic Games!"

How did Dory, the little blue regal tang fishy, say it in that dark and dangerous moment while trying to find Nemo? It seems that I remember her charging me to "Just keep swimmin' — just keep swimmin'!"

And that's precisely what this guy with the thirty-two inch waistline is going to do. I'm going to keep swimmin'.

For God has not given up on the Church today. And He's looking for some thirty-two inch waistlines who will keep going even when the road gets narrow, the way rocky, and the denim heavy.

Here's to a life of incorrigible cheerfulness, rejoicing always, and giving thanks in all things.

After all, isn't that "the will of God in Christ Jesus concerning us"?[*]

So, I for one am planning on doing just that.

I'd love for you to join me.

---

[*] 1 Thessalonians 5:18

ABOUT THE AUTHOR

There were three things growing up that Eric Ludy declared he would never become: a teacher, a missionary, and a pastor. He became all three. In a vain attempt to gain some credibility he also became a writer. But seventeen books later, he's admitted that this plan backfired big time—the messages contained in his books have led to more scorn than the other three combined. Ludy is the president of Ellerslie Mission Society, the teaching pastor at the Church at Ellerslie, and the lead instructor in the Ellerslie Discipleship Training. He descended from seven generations of pastors, is totally uncool, somewhat skinny, and in Japan supposedly his last name means "nerd." But, that said, he is clothed in the shed blood of His beloved Savior; Leslie, his wife of twenty years, still laughs at his jokes; and his six kids think he is Superman (or at least Clark Kent). So, all is well with the author of this book. He calls Windsor, Colorado home, but longs for his real home in heaven where being a "fool for Christ" finally will be realized to be the most brilliant life-decision any human has ever made.

EricLudy.com

MORE BOOKS FROM ERIC LUDY

Romance, Relationships, & Purity
When God Writes Your Love Story
When Dreams Come True
Meet Mr. Smith
A Perfect Wedding
The First 90 Days of Marriage
Teaching True Love to a Sex-at-13 Generation
It Takes a Gentleman and a Lady

Godly Manhood
God's Gift to Women

Christian Living & Discipleship
When God Writes Your Life Story
The Bravehearted Gospel
Heroism

Prayer
Wrestling Prayer

Memoirs & Confessions
Are These Really My Pants?
Evolution of the Pterodactyl
The Bold Return of the Dunces
Fingerprints of Grace

EricLudy.com

DISCOVER MORE FROM THE AUTHOR

SERMONS
Unashamed Gospel Thunder.
Listen now: Ellerslie.com/sermons

CONFERENCES
Come expectant. Leave transformed.
Learn more: Ellerslie.com/conferences

DISCIPLESHIP TRAINING
A set apart season to become firmly planted in Christ.
Learn more: Ellerslie.com/training

READ MORE FROM ERIC LUDY
EricLudy.com

www.ingramcontent.com/pod-product-compliance
Lightning Source LLC
Chambersburg PA
CBHW061300040426
42444CB00010B/2451